Twenty wins in Counting

I was scheduled to defend my XFA Welterweight Championship of the world for the record setting fourth time in San Diego, California. I was undefeated so far in my professional mixed martial arts career with a record of twenty wins and zero losses. I was in the locker room with my sensei, Brazilian Jiu-Jitsu sixth degree black belt, Professor Vitor Nogueria who was also a three time Brazilian Jiu-Jitsu World Champion.

He had been behind me my whole career. He was the one who agreed to train me exchange for food when I was too poor to afford classes to defend myself. In exchange for him feeding me and training me, I worked and cleaned the gym in Loira de Areia to the point that it was the cleanest school in the area and I put some of the maids to shame in Brazil and now I'm a Brazilian Jiu-Jitsu black belt and a former Brazilian Jiu-Jitsu World Champion.

"Are you ready?" the 5'11 older grey headed Brazilian man replied with a smile as he stood behind me wearing a white Adidas tracksuit with my walkout shirt underneath. He was none other than Professor Vitor Nogueria who was the driving force behind my mixed martial arts success.

He has always been there to corner me. I was his protégé and he always treated me like the son he never had. He was the one who promoted me to black belt in Judo after six years and five years after training in Brazilian Jiu-Jitsu. I didn't have any sponsors when I started out and now I'm one of the hottest mixed martial artist to ever come out of Brazil.

He smiled in approval as he checked my gloves one last time before I heard a knock on the door to let me know that it was time for me to come out and do my thing.

I nodded before he put my diamond encrusted gold XFA Lightweight Grand Prix Championship and my rose gold XFA Welterweight Championship belts around my waist before he tapped me on the shower and the security guards surrounded us as we walked towards the stage and waited patiently for my theme to come on.

The more that I thought about it, the more I got a little nervous about fighting against my opponent. Timmy Wong was a deadly knockout artist. He was like an Asian Mike Tyson with scary knockout power. He was always looking for the one punch knockout and refused to go down because he had an iron chin. He had gotten a hundred punches to the face and came back and knocked out some guy with one punch to win the XFA Lightweight Championship.

The lights in the arena of 13,000 people dimmed as the sight of red, white, and light blue lights flashed through the arena as the sound of "Cowboys from Hell" by Pantera started playing in the arena. The deafening response for me became well known as I through the curtains and smiled at the crowd. I raised both of my inked up arms and five massive explosions went off before I walked down the ramp while I shook hands with the fans. As I reached the cage, I took off both of my championship belts before I peeled off my walkout tee to show off my chiseled frame. The referee checked my gloves before I had my mouth guard put in while I had Vaseline applied to my face. I got the okay as I hugged my Professor Nogueria before I entered the cage for the twenty-first time and went to my neutral corner before I got ready to defend my title.

"This is the moment you have all been waiting for! This is the main event and it is for the XFA Welterweight Championship!" exclaimed the ring announcer as the crowd started cheering.

"In the blue corner in the blue shorts. He is the challenger from Hong Kong, China. He stands at five feet, eight inches tall and weighing in at one hundred and sixty-seven pounds. He has a fighting background in boxing and Tae Kwon Do where he is a third degree black belt. He holds a record of seventeen wins and four losses with fifteen of them by the way of knockout. He is the former XFA Interim Lightweight Champion. He is Timmy Wong!" Exclaimed the ring announcer before the crowd cheered and booed the bald headed durable knockout artist that reminded me of a chubby Shoalin Monk looking fighter.

"And in the red corner in the black shorts from Loira de Areia, Brazil! He stands at six feet, one inch tall and weighed in at one hundred and sixty-five pounds. He has a fighting background in Brazilian Jiu-Jitsu and Judo where he is a black belt in both disciplines. He holds an undefeated record of twenty wins and zero losses with all twenty of them by the way of submission with all of them ending in the first round. He is the current reigning and defending XFA Welterweight Champion of the World and the XFA Lightweight Grand Prix Winner. He is the undefeated champion. He is Julho 'Cobra' Damm!" exclaimed the ring announcer before the crowd went into an uproar before the referee motioned for us to come to the center of the cage for the championship fight.

"I have went over the rules with the both of you in the locker rooms. Remember to follow my rules at all times and remember this is for the belt. Punch gloves if you would like to do so and go back to your neutral corners so that we can get this fight started." exclaimed the referee as we shook hands before we both went back to our neutral corners before the referee called for the bell to start the fight.

The crowd started cheering as we both came to the center of the cage and he started the fight off with a random feint jab and busted out a spinning back kick that narrowly missed my head. Striking never was my specialty, but I did enough to just get by. I stepped to the side and threw a kick of my own that connected to the temple as I stepped back to the side to keep from getting into his striking range. He shot in and tried to take me down, but I sprawled out of it before I hooked his arm and took him down with a judo throw that took him to the ground as I held onto his arm to the delight of the crowd as he tried to fight off my submission attempt. He rolled onto his hands and knees before I rolled onto my back while I still held onto his arm before I wrapped my legs around his upper chest region and trapped him in my open guard as the crowd kept cheering for me. I kept my legs free while he tried to weasel his way out and I moved for better positioning, but that only pulled him deeper into my trap before I threw my leg over his shoulder and wrapped my legs together to lock him in my trademark triangle choke to nullify any of his chances for escaping. He was trying his best to slip out, but failed miserably. I could feel his body going limp before I heard the referee to call for the bell to end the fight to give me my twenty first victory.

After I turned him loose and stood up to my feet, I took my ponytail out and flipped my hair back before my wavy strands flowed down and covered my shoulder blades before I got a giant hug from my sensei as he handed me my walkout tee and Lightweight Grand Prix

Championship belt to put on before I was called to the center of the cage to hear the results from the match I had just won.

"The winner of this match going into the first round at one minute and fifteen seconds by the way of triangle choke tap out submission and still the XFA Welterweight Champion of the World! Julho 'Cobra' Damm!" exclaimed the announcer before the referee placed the championship belt around my waist for the fifth time in my career.

"Julho, you have just defended your belt for the fourth time in your career against the former Lightweight Champion, Timmy Wong. You have just snapped his five fight win streak with a nasty triangle choke. You made him look like an amateur and threw him around like a rag doll. You are the first person to ever submit him and you are still undefeated with twenty-one victories. What are your words on this fight?" asked the cage side announcer.

"Well Paul was a far from easy fight. He caught me off guard with his striking at first. He was a dominant champion, and he is one of the best fighters out there. He just came into my world and played my game and lost. I was the one who played blackjacked and got the perfect twenty-one. I'm thankful to God for giving me the strength to do everything that I do, and I'm looking forward to my next fight." I replied as I shook hands with Timmy Wong before I left the cage with my sensei.

Late Night Special

I had just defended my belt for the fourth time in record time. I had submitted Wong who I knew was going to be wondering about. He was one of my hardest opponents that I had to look out for since he was one hell of a striker along with knowing that he is a former champion. I know that he could have knocked me out if he had connected with one flush strike, but at the same time, I know that he was no match for me on the ground.

I was doing right at a hundred miles per hour in my brand new BMW M6 as I shot down the interstate. The song of Korn shot through my speakers as I started to calm down off my adrenaline rush. I was not the one who went out to the club after I celebrated with my camp. I was in a one man camp that was focused primary on Brazilian Jiu-Jitsu and Judo since I was a Brazilian Jiu-Jitsu purist who focused on taking the opponent to the ground before I went for a submission.

I was only a couple of minutes from my house, and I could not wait to get there. I dropped off Professor Nogueria at his house since he told me that he wanted out of the gym that he held ownership in that had just over three hundred and fifty students that come religiously.

As I looked up and pulled into my driveway before I rolled to a stop in front of my four bedroom, three bedroom house in the expensive upscale neighborhood in San Diego, California. As the garage door opened, I saw my oversized sport bike and my wife's green 2003 Buick LeSabre that she had when we first met. I rolled to a stop beside my wife's car before I stepped out before I grabbed my championship belts and watched the garage door close before I headed upstairs to see if I could find my wife.

I placed my championship belt inside of the trophy cabinet that I had just defended as I placed it alongside the other four belts that looked just like it. I placed the Grand Prix title on top of the case that I always had with me since I had to never defend that championship belt since it was a tournament that I had won.

I took a deep breath as I took off my hoody and kicked off my slides before I tossed my keys into the candy dish before I headed upstairs to find my wife.

The reason that she was never at my fights was because she did not support violence. She knows that's how I made a living, but she refused to come to see me fight. It was heartbreaking, but at the same time, she was the first girl that I had ever dated that did not want to come to support me in my line of work.

As soon as I walked into our bedroom, my lovely wife of the past three years, Melanie Berry-Damm was on the queen sized bed that we shared together.

I can remember what it was like when I first met her. I was doing some promotional work in Greenville, South Carolina. She was working for some kind of marketing firm that was linked to one of my sponsors. She was 25 at the time and I had just turned 19 so there was some space between us, but I was still doing pretty well for myself. It wasn't long before we started dating, got married, and moved to San Diego and we have been living that way ever since.

She was looking lovely. She had been through a lot, but she was still looking as gorgeous as usual. I could tell that she had been outside enjoying the sun because she had a bit of a tan to accent her beautiful body. She was stood right at 5'7 and weighed maybe a hundred and forty-five pounds. She had her hair in a brunette short pixie that had started to grow out a little bit. She had bright green eyes and an even brighter smile that always lit up the room, but today, I could not help but to lust over the way she was looking.

She was wearing this sexy little lime green corset outfit that magnified and accented her 34C breast that was still perkier than ever. She was probably about a 27 in the waist and about a 34 in the hips because she didn't have the biggest ass, but it was cute and a nice shape to it with just enough to smack.

"Hey sexy, I saw how the fight went. First round submission champ." she replied with a smile before I could help but to flash my million dollar smile and kiss her on the lips as I held her close to me. I gave her a nice playful spanking before I grabbed that nice bubble but of hers as she let a sensual moan escape before I felt her kiss me back aggressively.

She didn't hesitate to strip me down to my birthday suit in the most seductively way ever. As she took my clothes off, she kissed all over my muscular frame while I stood still like a pole as my seductive stripper did all the work before she grabbed me just below the base of my huge erection and pulled me close to her before I watched her run her stroke me a few times before she took my massive head deep inside of her mouth.

As much as we have been together, I still loved her with all of my heart. She was a virgin when I met her and I loved her to pieces. The one thing she could not do was suck a dick.

She was one of those what most people would call a "prude" but at the same time, she still tried her best. While she was bobbing up and down on me, I could feel her teeth scraping up against the sides of my shaft as I played along and like I was enjoying it while it was really patient with her. She pumped my shaft forcefully in a way that I could somewhat enjoy and the more that I tried to coach her, it seemed like she was not trying to get any better. Most of the time, I would skip oral and just get down to business.

I closed my eyes and ran my hands through her hair as I felt her trying to go down on me and get deeper with each thrust before she wrapped her tongue around my shaft as I felt her run her teeth up both sides of my shaft that made me shake my head in disbelief. I looked down at her as she looked up at me with those innocent eyes of hers before I put on a fake smile and let out a fake moan as if I was enjoying it before I pulled my shaft all the way out before I felt her kiss the tip of it so that I could get down to business with her.

She was always trying to get into her favorite position which was missionary. I tried to coax her into different positions, but she was so content on this one where I had to do all of the work. I was doing my best to keep myself calm as I spanked her playfully before she laid down on her back and eased her lime green thong off before she spread her legs and gave me a peak at her neatly trimmed bush. I would try to go down on her even if she was against it most of the time, but I was pretty tired after the fight so I didn't want to fight with her tonight while I was rock hard.

I stroked myself a couple of times before I pushed all 12 inches of me between the small slit between her legs as the two moist folds begged for mercy. She let out a loud gasp before I pulled her close to me and pinned her knees to her chest before I slowly started to inch my way inside of her before I started giving it to her.

"Oh yeah baby! That feels so good!" she moaned as she reached up and ran her hands over my chiseled chest and abs before I started pumping her while I watched her run her hands over her perky breast before she freed them from their cage while I looked down at her hard pinkish nipples that bounced freely with each time I pushed it deep inside of her. I was not even all the way in and she was screaming out in pain as she enjoyed the pleasure that she was receiving from me before I picked her hips off the bed and pounded her like a prisoner that had just got his freedom and she was the first woman that was willing to give him some. I was fucking her like a madman while I made sure that she was going to feel every bit of this tomorrow. I wanted to make up for the awful blowjob that she had given me. I was going to demolish her so hard that her walls were going to be needing a week to heal from the abuse that I was giving her! Each time I slammed it deep inside of her it sounded like a crack of thunder each time our thrust met each other's. She might have been resting all day, but at the same time, I know that she was going to be sorer than I was in the morning. I watched as a faint red tint covered her pale body with freckles in various places while I continued to give it to her tight white pussy. As I pulled out almost all the way, I pushed myself deep inside of her before I watched her jerk a couple of times before I went back to giving it to her. From the way that her body went limp as she started trembling to let me know that she had gotten hers before I tried my best to hold out after a couple of more hard thrust before my thickening erection exploded with three ropes of cum deep inside of her prudeness.

"That was lovely baby." she told me with a smile before she stood up and headed to the bathroom to take a shower. I wiped myself off with a couple of baby wipes and tossed them into the trash as I thought about how she was going to take it when I told her what I was going to do.

Press Conference

Roughly twenty-one hours later, I sat at the table with both of my championship belts sitting in front of me. I adjusted my pink necktie as I looked into the crowd of about three thousand spectators.

Paul was sitting right beside me and he had bruises and stitches from the beating I had given him last night. We were both dressed for the occasion since public relations was a part of the job. He was wearing a charcoal grey suit with a shite shirt and tie. I was wearing a navy blue pinstripe suit with a pink shirt and tie with a matching handkerchief. I barely had a scratch on me and let my hair hang down to enjoy the air as I got ready to hear the questions that our fans had in store for us.

"My question is for Paul Wong. What was your initial plan for beating Julho Damm last night?" asked the elderly white man who was in the front row that looked like he had on a Vietnam War veteran hat as he awaited the answer.

"My plan was to either keep the fight standing, or if the fight went to the ground, try my best to pass his guard or ground and pound him out to get the knockout." my opponent replied as I nodded in agreement since that was a pretty good idea.

"My question is for the champion. What was the hardest part about training for the fight against Paul Wong?" asked the younger looking redhead girl that looked like she belonged in a library instead of a mixed martial arts audience.

"Well to be honest, it would have to have been his heavy Tae Kwon Do background. In my career, I had to fight against mainly wrestlers, Muay Thai boxers, or boxers in general and other fellow grapplers. Tae Kwon Do had a variety of strikes that are not exactly easy to counter, so yeah that's the hardest part for me." I replied as I looked around at the crowd.

"My question is for Paul Wong. Are you going to stay in the welterweight divison, or are you going back to the lightweight division?" asked the middle aged dark headed man that reminded me of a broke man's Sylvester Stallone.

"I'll just jump back and forth for now to stay active since I walk around at one hundred and sixty pounds in general." he replied as I smiled lightly.

"Well that's a relief. I'm not much for choking you out anyway." I retorted as the crowd started laughing a little bit.

"And what's that supposed to mean?" he asked as he looked over at me.

"Because you are the fifth Asian I have choked out back to back in my mixed martial arts career. I don't want people to get the wrong impression and try to get me charged with a hate crime." I replied as the crowd went into hysterics as they called for the press conference to come to an end.

Then we both stood up and shook hands before the crowd cheered for the both of us. I picked up both of my championship belts and threw them over my broad shoulders before I walked down from the stage and shook hands with some of my loyal and supportive fans before I signed a few autographs. I signed a few shirts and took some pictures before the CEO, Tim Watts walked up to me and Paul.

"Congrats on a job well done. You guys did amazing with the pay-per-view buys." he replied as he handed Paul a check for half a million dollars. I was given a check for right at three and half million. *This was my biggest check I had ever recieved with the promotion.*

As security walked us to our cars, Paul jumped inside of his 2009 Ford F-150 pick-up truck before he jumped in and started the engine. I hit the unlock button on my keypad and the engine started to my M6. The truck flew open before I placed both of my championship belts in the trunk. I looked over and saw Paul waving at me before he sped off on his way. I waved back as I hopped inside of my car and added up the numbers of how I had made so much money.

I did pretty well. I had half a million to show. I had made half a million to win. I got another hundred grand for the best submission of the night. I got another hundred grand for the best fight of the night. The rest was my percentage of the pay-per-view sales which looked really good to me as I headed back to the house so that I could give my wife the good news.

House Divided

After I had got home from a grueling session with Professor Nogueria, I was sore. I had done weightlifting and Brazilian Jiu-Jitsu with him. Tomorrow was going to be cardio and judo so I had my body on a strict workout and diet.

I went upstairs to go to the bathroom and run a warm shower. I was sore and the warm bubble bath as the sound of some *Mya "Man in My Life"* played over the radio while my hair flowed under the waterfall while I thought about what I was going to tell Melanie.

Melanie had been through a lot honestly. She had been through a lot more than I had ever expected. She had been depressed for a while along with dealing with some bodily injuries that she could not help. After she had been in the car wreck, she had not been the same. I told her to stay home and I would take care of her, but she was so used to working that it didn't help. It was like telling a crackhead that a small hit would not be any good to him or her. Once she got back to work, it came back on her and she was depressed from the workload at work and one day she came home with all of her hair cut off and it was the only thing that had kept her from committing sucicide with was sad to hear. She even walked out on me a couple of times to be with her family, but I had my doubts the whole time because after she came home, things had not been the same. I still love her, but my heart aches and to this day I honestly have no idea what's going on with her.

As I stepped out of the shower and dried myself off, I pulled my hair back into a ponytail and gave myself a quick shave before I cleaned myself off. I threw on a pair of basketball shorts and a green wifebeater before I walked into our bedroom to tell her the news that I had for her.

"Hey Jules, what are you up to?" she asked before I walked up to her and hugged her before I kissed her on the lips before we snuggled up on the sofa in our bedroom together. I closed my eyes and held her close to me as I tried to forget about the things in our past.

"I was doing some thinking. You know that I'm from Brazil and everything right?" I asked as she nodded in agreement. "Okay with that being said as you know my grandfather died last year and he left me his beach house. You know that house is part of my heritage and on top of that, it's worth three million Brazilian Reals or one and a half million dollars in United States funds. I'm drained in America and a bit homesick. As much as I love San Diego, I know that I have to do what I have to do."

"Baby, is everything okay?" she asked as she looked at me while she lied beside me wearing a pair of my baggy black loungepants and a black tank top as she ate on a banana.

"Yeah, I really want to go back to Brazil." I told her truthfully as she shook her head in disagreement.

"I know that you do, but I love it here." she whined lightly since I know that it's not going to be easy talking this stubborn mule into moving out of the United States.

"Master Nogueria is for the idea as well. It will be benefitical to my training as well." I replied as she tried to negotiate with me to keep me from moving.

"Okay, if that's what you want to do, I'm fine with it, but please don't have too much for fun." she told me in regards to me cheating on her in the past.

"Okay, great." I replied as I kissed my lovely and supportive wife on the lips and held her close to me.

"Baby, promise me that you will call me every night to make sure that you are okay." she told me as I looked deep into her eyes.

"Promise." I replied as I hugged her despite all the things that we have been through as if I was never going to see her again.

Long Flight Alone

I was starting to think about everything that was going on. I was on top of my game in my mixed martial arts career. I had two million dollar homes in two different countries. I had a wife that hated my guts even if she said that she loved me and sold both of my cars and made right at a hundred grand in total so now I have the fun part of picking out the cars down here to put my garage.

As I looked out the hotel window, I thought about how the water had damaged the property and Professor Nogueria was already there to help me with some of the things and he was living inside of his gym which I know saved him some money.

I had confirmed my car rental and got my hotel room taken care of the XFA which was a blessing. I didn't have anything to bring with me to the house in Brazil except for my championship belts, electronic devices, clothes, and money since I didn't have too many valuable things to worry about. *I had everything on the plane which was a relief.*

I started to get settled in and they told me that it would take two months to get everything taken of, but the insurance was covering it so I was happy.

I had texted my wife to let her know that I was at the hotel in Loira de Areia, Brazil. I was debating if I was going to go to the gym and get in a quick workout or if I was going to relax in the hotel room and order room service and watch TV. *It was only two thirty so the day was still young and I was not sure what was going to happen next on my end.*

I heard a loud knock on the door before I waited patiently and heard someone say housekeeping before my door came open. I was still lying in bed as the footsteps started to get a little louder inside of my tenth floor penthouse suite at the hotel room that was the last one on the floor so I guess that whoever it was saved the best for last.

As I looked up and saw what the housekeeper looked like, my mouth nearly dropped at how beautiful she was. *I know that there was no way that I could think clearly because half of the blood in my body was down in my pants and what's left of my brain was full of dirty and nasty thoughts.*

She had to have been in her mid to late twenties from the way that she looked. She had a nice smooth tanned complexion and she was the true definition of a Brazilian Maid. The ones that the guys jacked off to in the movies and magazines had nothing on this banging Mamacita. Her beauty was like a stun gun that neutralized my body and kept me from moving as I forgot how to even move when I locked eyes with her.

The 5'2 beauty stood in front of me as I looked at all one hundred and forty-five pounds of her. She had her hair cut into a bob with a bit of a red tint to it. She had light green eyes that were starting right through me. They were so hypnotic that she was able to see exactly what was on my mind and I was under her spell. She had about a 36C chest, roughly a 24 inch waist and a nice 38 inch ass because that thing stuck out like a shelf in her uniform that did her body no mercy. She was wearing a pink top and bottoms that were a little snug and I know that she looked even better without those clothes on. As she licked her luscious full lips, I could only imagine what she was thinking about as she got closer to me.

"Hey, did you hear me when I knocked?" she asked curiously as I sat up and flipped my hair back before I stood up in my black workout pants and tight fitting V neck white tee before I looked down at her.

"Maybe I was waiting to see if you was worth the wait and you definitely were." I replied as I scanned her from head to toe as she moved her body seductively.

"I'm Julho, what's your name?" I asked.

"I'm Yolanda. Are you Julho Damm, the cage fighter?" she asked as she looked at my championship belts.

"Yeah that would be me. I'm basically chilling here for now until I get my house here straightened out since I'm moving back here." I told her as she smiled before she finished cleaning up my room and replaced my closet with new towels and changed the sheets on my bed.

"It's almost time for me to get off. I will catch you later because I don't want to get in trouble." she told me before she strutted away from me before she looked back and saw that I was still eyeing her and she gave me a smile and a flirtatious wave before she walked out of my life temporary. *Damn, I wish that tomorrow would hurry up so that I could see her again.*

Back to Basics

It felt good to be training back at home again. I had been rolling with Professor Nogueria as I tried to blow off some steam from the way that my wife had been treating me before I had left to go to Brazil.

I was pumped about fighting in ADCC. I got the email with the invite and I had already prequalified. They were bringing the competition to Loira de Areia for the first time and I could not be happier. I wanted that title for a while and I was not going to rest until I got to do what I had wanted to do.

I took out my frustration on my longtime sensei as he trained me with some new moves that I had not been accustomed to using on a regular basis. I was so used to training that gym in San Diego but to be back in Loira de Areia was an amazing feeling.

Training with a three time world champion and former ADCC Champion was pretty cool as well. He has some children and all of them have decorated martial arts careers as well, even if some of them found other careers of interest that grabbed their attention. The thing is, if they want to spend the night at Professor Nogueria' s house, they have to roll with him and however many times they make him tap is how many weeks they can stay with him, and he is not going to go easy on anyone.

I know that for a fact.

I was working on my open guard some more which was my favorite grappling position to use whenever I was on the ground trying to take someone out. Usually I would attempt a triangle choke which was my favorite or go for an armbar. For me, I would go for whichever one was the most convenient at the moment.

We were both going back and forth tapping each other out. Since we were both black belts in Judo, we were both throwing each other around like ragdolls, then going in for the submission which was convenient for the both of us. The only ones that were ever able to tap me were some of his sons when I was an under ranking belt, but I have got my revenge on them and made them all tapped to the modified anaconda choke that I learned from their father.

Since it was coming close to the end of our training practice for the day, I wanted to bring out all the stops since I knew that I had another fight coming up. I refused to let anyone take my belt and I was going to choke out anyone that was going to try and get in my way.

I hit a couple of leg trip takedowns before I made him land face first to the mat before I took his back. I wrapped my legs around his waist as he held onto my wrist and started to turn before he free himself from my legs that were wrapped around his waist. I eased to my feet as I used my other arm and wrapped it around his neck before I grabbed my wrist and squatted down on his shoulder before I got him in a Peruvian necktie that made him tap out to my submission.

"That was great Julho." he told me as I helped him up to his feet before I took a deep breath and hugged him before we hit the showers.

A lot of things were going through my mind at the moment. As the water came over my body, I thought about how beautiful my housekeeper was and how cool it would be to have her as a live in maid while my wife was in the United States. Melanie already made me want to leave her anyway and it was not like she had anything for her except for the fact she is married to me. I wanted to leave her a while back, and as I looked at my wedding ring, I thought about how it was becoming just a piece of overpriced metal than it was a symbol of love.

Club Midnight Special

With the crazy training camps and all of the hell I had been through with my wife, I needed to get the edge off. I was in a country full of beautiful women and the more that I talked to my wife, the worst my headache got.

I was looking forward to my fight tomorrow. I was going to be fighting against Hector Castillo-Martinez which was not going to be an easy fight, but I was looking forward to it more than anything.

I was cruising around in my rented black Dodge Ram 1500 Quad Cab as I headed in route to the club. I was still debating what I was going to put in the garage alongside my tricked out motorcycle. I had a couple of ideas, but I will wait until I go to the dealership and see what my choices are with a hundred grand in my pocket.

As the sound of some old school Ludacris thumped from the speakers, I cruised around while I was thinking of a chill place to relax at. I remembered there was this club I used to go to all the time before I went to the United States by the name of Club Midnight. *If I had a dollar for everytime I got laid here, I would have enough money to put Donald Trump to shame.*

I knew the owner and I had a lifetime V.I.P. membership with the company and who didn't know who I was. I pulled into the parking lot and cut the engine before I stepped out in a pair of black cargos, a light blue stonewashed teeshirt and a pair of flip flops with my freshly done cornrows hanging down my back. I had on a solid diamond watch and a matching bracelet. I looked at my wedding band and shook my head before I went past the line and hugged a few of the people in the line and shook hands. I took a few pictures before I signed some autographs and shook hands with the bouncer before I went inside of the place that I held a five percent stake in.

The familiar atmosphere greeted me as I walked through the crowd of recent high school grads and college students that made up a huge percentage of the party atmosphere. I had accomplished a couple of goals that I had been trying to achieve within my career. I needed to try my best to have some fun and get the edge off without trying my best to get myself injured.

I surfed through the crowd as I made my way onto the dance floor and I knew that I could not dance my way out of a wet paper bag. The sound of some upbeat techno music played over the sound system as I moved along to the beat and tried to become one with the melody. I felt a couple of girls dance up on me as I ran my hands over their silhouette and a couple of girls backed it up for me to my delight, but hey, at the day, I'm still a well known professional athlete from the area so you know that the ladies was going to show me some love.

I watched this one girl dance up against me and the nicest ass in these tightest short white dress came up against my crotch. I didn't care who it was because this body was amazing and I got down low with the girl on the dance floor as my rock hard erection buried itself deep inside of her ass crack as she leaned back and moaned sensually in my ear before I ran my hands over her flat stomach and held her close to me.

"What's your name sexy?" I asked as sucked on her earlobe lightly as her sweet smelling perfume filled my nostrils and me feel some kind of a way as I refused to elave this club without getting to know her a little bit better.

"Yolanda," she whispered as she kissed me on the cheek and I looked down at her to see that she was my maid from the other day.

"Damn girl, you look good without your maid outfit on." I told her as I knew that there was more to the beautiful woman that met the eye.

"Why thank you Senhor Damm." she replied in a playful tone as she ran her hand against my jawline while I blew a warm stream of air against the side of her neck before I bit her lightly on the neck in the dinly lit room.

"Did you drive here?" she asked as she gyrated lightly against my foot long piece of meat.

"Yeah," I replied as she looked up at me with a smile.

"Good, then let's get the fuck out of here." she suggested as I nodded in agreement before we made our way through the club and headed outside to the parking lot.

I unlocked my rented Ram as we both hopped inside before I started the engine and left the club without looking back.

Before I was out of the parking lot good, she had already reached over and massaged my tool through my shorts before she undid my pants and fished it out and smiled in delight at how big I was.

'Damn papi, are you going to let me taste it?" she asked playfully as she wrapped her pierced tongue around my huge head a couple to times before she started to suck on it seductively as she looked up at me with those sexy green eyes of hers. She was not playing around as she started to deeper on me with each thrust as she wrapped her tongue around me while she pumped my massive shaft to my delight. I had one had on the wheel and the other hand on the back of her head as I tried to control the pace of how good she was handling my knob while pools of saliva were forming at my bass and I could not stop the tension between us even if I wanted to. She was coming up every so often just to catch her breath as she kept picking up the pace and controlling me. She had both hands around my shaft while I was trying my hardest to keep my eyes open as I went down the street at around eighty miles per hour while my rock hard cock shivered in her mouth as I clenched my ass cheeks together while I held it together.

"Pull over, I gotta have this dick inside of me." she told me as she came up and motioned for me to pull over behind the doctor's office which I quickly agreed to before I rolled to a stop behind her destination as I cut the engine. She didn't waist anytime jumping out of the truck as I stepped out of my shorts and she bent over as she pulled her dress up the back and showed me that she hang on a black, pink, and white striped thong that I quickly snatched to the side so that I could press my head between her two tight satin like folds that tensed up around my cock.

"Ah Julho! You're so fucking big!" she exclaimed as she looked over her shoulder as I pushed my way deeper inside of her as I started working it in and out of her. I watched as she tensed up as I rested my hands on her shapely hips as I hit the corners while I gave it to her to a nice smooth rhythm that she quickly caught onto as I kept getting deeper inside of her with each thrust. She was screaming out some loud shrieks of pleasure as I controlled her while I picked up the pace. She was holding onto the front of the truck as I started pounding her deep and hard from the back while I was making her wish that she had never left me in my hotel room without giving me the slightest bit of pleasure. I watched as she struggled to stand on her own two feet while I was controlling her and she managed to stay on for the ride in this position before she pushed me on and grabbed my shaft as she motioned for me to sit down on the side step on the truck and I did so before she squatted down on me and took me deep inside.

"Oh yeah! That feels so good! Do you like it when I ride that big black dick baby! Do you love it when I'm in control like that! Do you want me to show you how much I love having that dick inside of me! Does that feel good to you! How do you like that!" she exclaimed as she reached up and undid the tie behind her neck and watched them freefall to her waist as I fucked her hard from the bottom while she rode the hell out of my massive dick. I was resting my hands on her shapely hips while she made her body one with her personal melody as I felt my balls being coated with her creamy white liquids on my cock as I refused to give her a second to relax. I ran my hands over her sweaty curvy frame while I was trying my best to stay up with her as she closed her legs and pulled my arms around her waist and held me close to her before I felt a huge rush come over body a couple of times before she calmed down and held me deep inside of her. I felt my cock starting to grow inside of her as I felt myself filled her up with a couple of ropes of cum as she dropped her head in pleasure.

"Shit!" she exclaimed as she stood up and walked off lightly as she tried to hold onto the side of the door while I was fixing my clothes.

"Do you need me to drop you off at the club?" I asked as she nodded before I hopped in the truck and she crawled in beside me before I started the engine and headed on my way back to the club.

"So how long are you staying at the hotel?" she asked.

"I'm here for another couple of weeks because my house is getting ready?" I replied as she saw the diamond ring on my finger.

"Are you married?" she asked curiously.

"More like an estranged marriage to be honest with you." I told her as she nodded in agreement.

'Do you love her?" she asked.

"I do, but she loves me from a far so it feels like we aren't even married." I replied as she smirked.

"Well married or not, I enjoyed my time with you." she told me with a smile as I pulled into the parking lot before she pointed to the older Honda in the parking lot before I smiled and she kissed me on the cheek before she hopped out of the truck and waved at me as she hopped into the car before she pulled out and I drove off behind her into the darkness to get ready for my fight tomorrow.

Fifth Title Defense

I was making history within the XFA. No one had ever made it past three title defenses within the promotion and I was going for my fifth title defense.

I was ready to take out my opponent. I was going up against the former Golden Gloves champion who was equally a good wrestler. I was finally able to go up against someone who wasn't Asian, and I was ready to make history within the promotion because I knew that I was going to not accept anything but a win against him.

As I took a couple of deep breaths as I headed to the arena, I closed my eyes and did a quick prayer before I walked inside of the arena to the sound of "Party Like A Rockstar" by The Shop Boyz which sounded like my current lifestyle yesterday.

As I came into the arena with both of my champion belts around my waist, I raised both of my arms and five explosions went off as I walked down the ramp and headed towards the cage. I shook hands with the fans until the referee stopped me. I handed my championship belts off before I took off my walkout tee and hat and shook off the effects from last night as I had the Vaseline quickly applied to my face. After my gloves were given the okay, I hugged Professor Nogueria before I went inside of the cage and got ready to handle my opponent and end his three fight win streak.

As I looked at my opponent, he smirked at me, but I didn't let him intimidate me. He was a stocky Mexican dude that looked like a black guy with good hair. He was covered in all kinds of hair and tattoos and I was ready to take down the former Golden Gloves and NCAA Wrestling Champion and show him that this is my house.

"This is the moment that you have all been waiting for! This is the main event and it's for the XFA Undisputed Welterweight Championship of the World!" the announcer exclaimed as the crowd began to die down.

"In the blue corner from Mexico City, Mexico. He stands at five nine, and weighed in at one hundred and seventy pounds. He has a fighting background in boxing and colliegate wrestling. He holds a professional record of sixteen wins and two losses, with fourteen of them by the way of knockout. He is the former XFA Interim Middleweight Champion. Give is up for Hector Castillo-Martinez!" exclaimed the ring announcer as the crowd began cheering for him a little bit as he tried to become a two division champion within the promotion.

"And in the red corner from Loira de Areia, Brazil! He stands at six feet, one inch tall and weighed in at one hundred and sixty-nine pounds! He has a fighting background in Judo and Brazilian Jiu-Jitsu where he has black belts in both disciplines. He holds a professional record of twenty-one wins and zero losses with all twenty-one of them finishing in the first round. He is the XFA Lightweight Grand Prix Champion and the current, reigning, and defending XFA Welterweight Champion going into his fifth title defense. Give it up for Julho"The Cobra" Damm!" exclaimed the ring announcer as the referee motioned for both of us to come to the center of the cage.

"I want a clean fight. Remember to protect yourself at all times. Remember this for the belt and follow my rules at all times. If there are no questions, punch gloves and go back to your neutral corner and let's do this." the referee replied as we punched gloves before we went back to our neutral corners. As soon as the referee called for the bell, the crowd came alive as we both came charging to the center of the cage.

We were both going hard against each other as he tried to finish me fast with a knockout punch, but I dodged both of them. I shook it off as I wrapped my arms around his waist and hooked his leg and threw him to the ground with a fast judo throw that put him flat on his back. He was naturally bigger than me, and he used his upper body strength to launch me in the air before I held onto his wrist and landed on my feet and caught him with a couple of knees to the face, before I wrapped my arm around his neck and got him under the throat before I flipped him over me and wrapped my legs around his waist. I was going to try to finish him with a guillotine and he rolled onto his back in a way that I could not get him the way that I wanted. I know that he thought he had an opening, but I refused to let the submission go. I turned my legs loose before I stood to my feet and stepped over his shoulder before I torque downwards and got him with a rare Peruvian necktie and tapped him out to give him my twenty-second victory and the title.

As the crowd cheered for me, Professor Nogueria came in with not of my championship belts and hugged me. As soon as I put on my hat and walkout tee, the referee motioned for me to come to the center of the cage to hear the results of the fight.

"The winner of this match, going into the first round at one minute and twelve seconds by the way of submission and still champion, Julho "The Cobra" Damm!" exclaimed the ring announcer as Tim Watts placed my championship belt around my waist since I got a new one with every title defense.

"Julho, you dished out some knees and made quick work of Tito Martinez as you finished him off with a Peruvian Necktie. What is your opinion of how this fight went and defending your title for a fifth time?" the ring announcer asked me.

"Well the fight went the way that I wanted. I had wanted to get him with a guillotine, but as you could see, he defended that, but I got him with the Peruvian Necktie and I knew that it was all over. But with that being said, I am getting close to wiping out all of the contenders for my belt. I am always looking for new competition and I will be entering the XFA Welterweight Grand Prix Tournament and I will win and beat the undefeated king of the one hundred and eighty-five pound division and that's a promise!" I replied with a smile before I left the cage with Professor Nogueria and headed back on my way.

Post Fight Party

I was on top of the world. I had choked out Hector with a Peruvian necktie that scored me an extra hundred grand for the submission of the night. I was waiting on the paycheck to drop in my bank account as I headed back to my hotel room.

I was never the one to party, but I was calling it early tonight. I had my fun the night before the fight and now I'm living the high life. I had an eight digit salary at the end of the year and it was time for me to kick back, order room service and watch some TV since I haven't done that one since I got here.

I ordered some kind of Jet Li movie with English subtitles since I was not fluent in Chinese. I went ahead and got some dinner since I was a bit hungry after the weigh cut and the training camps.

I looked down at my phone and saw where my wife had called me and I didn't want to be bothered. I know that she saw the fight and just wanted me to retire. *Somethings never changed and honestly I didn't want to hear it.*

A couple of minutes later, the door opened and instead of it being one of the bell boys, it was Yolanda who I thought was off from work today. *I know that I must have seen her at my fight tonight in the audience.*

She came in wearing something a bit scandalous that made almost forget about my foot and my movie while I looked at her wearing a pair of black slacks, a chef choat and hat and some five inch heels as she batted her eyes at me before I closed the door behind her.

"Is that within regulation of the uniform standards here." I asked curiously as I watched her ass move back and forth in the loose fitting pants before she rolled my foot to the kitchen as I sat down at the table and she glanced at my championship belts and gloves that were a makeshift centerpiece.

"Is that all that you are worried about? What I'm wearing?" she asked as I could not help but to smirk at her playful gesture as I sat down and looked out the window at the beach before I focused my attention back to her before she picked the lid off the tray to show me what they had prepared for me.

"Since you are the highest profile client we have at the moment, the chef would not settle for sending you anything but the best." she told me as the aroma filled my nostrils. "We have as the main entree we have seasoned Kobe beef steak that is medium rare from the cows in Japan. On the side we have some steamed rice that is seasoned to perfection. We have some steamed mixed vegetables along with some Acai Berry on the side since we know that you don't drink."

I closed my eyes to enjoy the smell of it. After I got in a good sniff, I opened my eyes to see that she had taken off her hat and her chef coat so that I could get a good look at her before I saw the pants sit on her lowrise waist so that I could get a hint of her light blue lacy printed thong before I got ready to chow down.

As I eyed my dinner, she sliced up my foot for me as I saw that she fixed the fork so that I could get the first bite of food that send my mind to a million places.The food was so good and as she was feeding me, I grabbed my glass and took a sip of my drink as I watched her take the napkin and clean my face before I went continued to chow down on the food. I was running my eyes over the lustful beauty as I coninued to scann her from head to toe.

As I finished up my food, I stood up as she cleaned the crumbs from my face with her tongue before she kissed me on the lips and hugged me close to her before I kissed her passionately. She ran her hands over my cornrows while I was running my hands over her curvy body and over that nice round ass of hers while I felt her break the kiss of so that she could kiss her way over my neck before she kissed both of us down to our birthday suits while I noticed that she grabbed a knife and a pineapple as we went to the bedroom.

"Lay down on the bed. It's time for the champ to enjoy the ride after that fight you just one", she told me as I agreed reluctantly before she quickly sliced up the pineapple and watched the juice dripped over my body. I felt the cool liquid drip onto my crotch and she smiled as she placed the biggest chunk on top of my huge head and took her time with me. I was feeling the cold liquid coat my body as I saw various chunks placed in various places before I laid back and got a little more comfortable after she placed the knife back on the rolling cart and climbed onto the bed with me.

She licked it off some various places before she kissed her way all over me. I could not help but to smile as I felt her warm breath mix with the cold air and liquid on my body. She massaged the fruit juice into the skin of my sore body and my muscles relax as she took control of me while I ate the remainder of the delicious fruit off my body before I watched her place a piece in my mouth before I nibbled on the piece that we shared together before our tongues got into a passionate war with each other before I found my hands massaging her thick thighs while she was making me not want to leave her before I watched as she licked her way down to the piece that was on the tip of my massive head.

She was so creative with it. She was running her tongue around my swollen head as she teased my head before she turned over and squatted down on my face to show me that she hid the last piece of pineapple between her two moist folds that I felt my massive cock slide in and out of last night as I wrapped my muscular arms around her two thick thighs before she squatted down on my face and rode the hell out of my head as she dripped the juice onto my head before I watched her drop it low on my face while I was getting the pleasure of my life from her.

As she got deeper on me with each thrust as she bobbed up and down on me. I felt the tip of my toes tease the base of her asshole as she bobbed up and down on me. As she the sweet taste of her pussy mixed with pineapples sent my taste buds into another world while she sucked me violently while I was running my hands over her huge ass while she continued to give my dick a heavenly touch with her educated tongue while she grinded up against my face while I ran my tongue around her clit wildly before I felt her drop all of her weight on me before she shivered wildly ontop of me to let me know that she had gotten that O she had been trying to reach. I sucked hard on her fat pussy lips as she deepthroated me to make me tense up while I felt a stream of pussy juice coat my face as I licked her sweet taste off my lips before I gave her a second to regain her composure.

She didn't waste any time throwing her self over me before she mounted me and took my head deep inside of her before I rested my hands on that fat ass of hers while she rode the life out of me. She was moaning in pleasure as she fucked me like she was never going to be able to give it to me again. My cock was singing in pleasure while she refused to give me a second to breath. She was so fluid with her strokes as she bounced up and down on me while I was fucking her her hard from the bottom. She was screaming all kinds of comments in Portuguese. I was turning her ass into a conga drum while I fucked the shit out of that pussy that had been calling my name all day. I was pounding her so good and deep that I know she was feeling it in her stomache. She was so full of energy as she leaned down to kiss me on the lips to show me anything but a good time. She rested her feet on the ground and held onto my wrist as I watched her thick thighs echo off of mine while she came down and did her hips in some fast circles. When she dropped it low on me and took me all the way deep inside of her as a loud and passionate moan escaped as she felt me beginning to throb inside.

She looked at me with a smile as she hooked her legs under my thighs and bounced wildly on top of me before I grabbed that massive bunda of hers before she looked over her shoulder and watched that ass bounce on my cock before she reached to the heavens and took me all the way inside of her before I pulled her close to me and held her before I filled her up with four ropes of pleasure from my rock hard eruption."

"Damn Julho!" she exclaimed as she sat up and ran to the shower to clean herself off.

I sat up realizing I had cheated on my wife a couple of times in less than two days. I know that she was going to be mad and she is going to know something is up since I haven't called her back. *Well I'll deal with that in the morning.*

Wake Up to Hell

It was Sunday morning and the more I thought about it, the less I wanted to be bothered. I had just woke up at around eleven the afternoon as I realized that I never did call her back last night. I know that we are married and we talk on the phone every night before I go to sleep, but at the same time, she was still a royal pain the ass at the end of the day. *I know she is going to give me hell as soon as I pick up this phone and call her crazy ass back.*

As I reached over to grab my phone, and told it to call my wife who was becoming a stranger a little bit more by the day. I was feeling myself breaking away from her slowly since long distance relationships never worked for me, along with being halfway down the glove away from her. I was trying to imagine what she might be calling me about since she is usually in a bad mood and takes out her anger on me any chance that she gets to. On the forth ring, I heard her pick up to hear what she had to say.

"Hello." I replied.

"Hey Julho, what's up?" she asked in a bit of a perky tone which made me as happy as much as it scared me.

"I'm good, just waking up. Me and Professor Nogueria have been training for the Abu Dhabi tournament. What have you been up to?" I asked. *Technically I wasn't lying, but at the same time I was not telling her the full truth since I don't think she has been honest with me throughout the time we were together.*

"Oh okay, I'm good, just about to go back inside sine my break is almost over." she sighed.

"Oh okay, what do you have planned for today?" I asked as I went downstairs and headed towards the parking lot to see what was going on back at the house.

"Well I am getting some paperwork situated so that I can get myself situated. So are you dead serious about me coming to Brazil?" she asked.

"Yes I'm dead up serious. I have a house next to the beach and you don't have to work. I have everything ready for you. All you have to do is bring your beautiful face since I have everything situated." I puersuaded since I know that she was a bit on a stubborn side.

"Okay, I will think about it. I will take a vacation there, and if I like it, I'll stay. If not, I'm coming back home." she told me.

"Okay, that's fair." I replied with a sigh of relief since I know that she was coming to see me.

"With that being said, have you got your motorcycle yet?" she asked.

"I don't know yet. I'm headed back to the house to see if they have everything done yet." I told her as I hopped into the rental and started the engine.

"Okay cool, I will call you later on because I'm walking into my office." she told me. "I love you."

'I love you too." I replied truthfully as I blew her a kiss into the phone before I hung up and backed out of the parking space as I got ready to head on my way.

So she is finally coming to Brazil. I know that its a huge step and I know that she has enough personal days built up since she never misses work willing. She is probably hiding something, but at the same time, my nails aren't exactly clean either. I will worry about that later since I have more important things to handle at the moment.

Home Sweet Home

I was so glad to be going back to my childhood home for the first time in close to seven years. The house had been flooded out thanks to the last hurricane, but I had ten million dollars worth of insurance house so that just in case it came through again, I'm getting ten million and moving away from the water and selling the house to some kind of a developer for at least a million dollars.

I pulled into my driveway and cut the engine as I looked at my renovated house that I used to stay in on occasion when I was growing up during the holidays. I remember living with Master Nogueria and when my mom was going through rehab, I was always here over the weekends since I was not allowed to be in that enviroment. I know that I was not in the best living conditions, but I would not change it for the world. I might not have any friends, but I had millions of fans which was a great feeling.

I stepped out of the car and locked it behind me as I opened the front door to see that my house was just like the way I remembered it when I was a child. I had on the furniture replaced with the way that it looked before the storm had came through. Everything looked like the way that it did before and how the house is reinforced with materials that are able to stand up to pretty serious hurricane which is pretty cool.

I walked through the house and looked at the new floors and marble island in the middle of the kitchen. I was gad that I didn't have any neighbors close by the massive eight thousand square foot estate that was surrounded by an iron rod fence. Since I was the only grandchild and my mother was the only child, I got everything that belonged to him. I sent my mom his old school Buick since she needed the car more than I did at the time.

As I walked through the house, I looked at some of the pictures of what looked like a happy family compared to what it really was. My grandfather didn't really like me and since my dad wasn't in the picture, I was only allowed to come around during holidays. He was a stern older black man that didn't really start to give a damn about me until he saw that I had a chance to be the best in the world which I am today then he expressed an interest in me. He already had money from owning a percentage of a steel company that was sold and he got a couple of million off it. He gave my mother a hundred grand cash and she just smoked it up and the money that I was suppose to get went to pay her bills since she had no more money from her habit so I was just screwed all around until Professor Nogueria took me in and I can't thank him enough for that.

I had a new bed put in so that I could get a full night's sleep without the thoughts of having his bed under me. I did not want to relive those memories.

I loved the house overall. I had five bedrooms, three and half bathrooms, a three car garage and a view of the beach from looking out my bedroom window which was a warm feeling that I could never get enough of.

I had only one major renovation done. I had a trophy case put in the penthouse suite so that I could see all of my championship belts and Brazilian Jiu-Jitsu and Judo awards and medals. I had more than I could count and I refused to stop until my heart gave me the ultimate ultimatium to quit.

I went to the garage and saw the shipping crate with my motorcycle inside of it. I loved my 2001 Suzuki GSXR-1300rr that I had customized just for me. I had bought the massive bike after my first fight with the XFA and took half of it to make the bike my own. I had it lowered to the ground with a supercharger. I had it set up for nitrous along with a 240 back tire. I upgraded the engine a little bit and added a mean Brazilian flag paintjob that brought out the chrome on the bike.

I felt my phone vibrating and looked down to see that it was Yolanda calling me and I was curious about what she was up to.

"Hey what's up?" I asked.

"Nothing much, about to go on break, what are you doing?" she asked.

"I'm at home right now. What's up with you?" I asked.

"Let's meet up for lunch." she replied.

"Okay where and what's the time?" she asked.

"Let's say in fifteen minutes at the Locale restaraunt." she suggested.

"Okay, I'll see you there." I replied as I grabbed my motorcycle keys and took the bike off the kickstand as I walked the bike out of the garage and pulled the rental into the garage and closed it.

I started the bike up and revved it up a little bit since I hadn't rode it in close to a couple of years because of my training. I went to the end of the driveway and kicked into first gear as I headed off to see my petite Brazilian Mistress.

First Degree Burns

I had been training with Professor Nogueria like crazy for the ADCC tournament. I had been working on my strength training as well as my throws since I was going up against some real grappling heavy hitters. I know that I was goig to be in two different ivions and going to try to go gor the Openweight Division.

I was pulling ut all of the stops tonight. I was pulling off a modified open guard that Professor Nogueria was not as used to since he was closed guard master that I used to find trouble woth when I had first started out doing Brazilian Jiu-Jitsu.

I rolled and caught him in a front arm trapped guillotime as he shot in and tackled me to the ground as he went for a front arm lateral throw that sent me flying, but I still head onto the submission. He was a strong man for his age and so technical with his approach as he went from a leglock of his own. He was always a crafty martial artist, and he went for a rolling heelhook that I quickly managed to slide my foot free from before I managed to roll into an angled D'Arce choke before I turned my shoulder upwards. He tried his best to fight it off as I flattened myself out with a wrestler's sprawl before I made him tap out to my submission hold.

After I released the submission hold, I helped him up to his feet before I gave him a giant hug and he accepted my gesture of sportsmanship as we both walked over our duffle bags and started drinking some water.

"What do you think of the next house?" He asked as he downed half a bottle of Powerade and I took a deep breath.

"It's pretty nice. I'm getting some things situated, but I have already moved in. I just have to get the cars to fill up the garage." I told him as he nodded.

"Julho, you have been doing an excellent job with your Brazilian Jiu-Jitsu. You are the last of a dying breed. You are one of the last Brazilian Jiu-Jitsu purist, the martial art that made mixed martial arts what is today before all of the sponsors and the mainstream appeal. You have earned your first degree black belt in Brazilian Jiu-Jitsu." he told me as he handed me the certificate and the black belt that he told me that I had worked so hard to get.

I had been training so hard in mixed martial arts. I had achieved my goal of getting the first degree black belt in Brazilian Jiu-Jitsu after training in twelve years. I had gotten my black belt in Judo after training for six and half years and my black belt in Brazilian Jiu-Jitsu for training at round four and a half years. I had been fighting professionally for just over five years and I was a two time world champion and hoping to make it a three time champion after I won the tournament. I had been a Brazilian Jiu-Jitsu World Champion and a former Judo champion. I might not be as decorated in Judo, but at the same time, I still find it to be a valuable part of my arsenal.

I reached into my bag and handed Professor Nogueria a set of house keys.

"You have been a huge part of my life and I can't think you enough. I have lived with you in the back of the gym when times were my hardest. I would like to repay you by giving you the keys to the house that is right in front of mine." I told him as he broke down crying to let me know how much that meant to him.

He had never had a house growing up. He had to choose between living in a house or running his school and he chose the hard knock life. He made himself a legend and I wanted to show the 6th degree Brazilian Jiu-Jitsu black belt that hard work does pay off. *I felt like my father figure was the only person worthy of being my neighbor since he was the only person on this side of the world that I had ever trusted.*

Going Out with a Bang

"OH SHIT JULHO! OH YEAH BABY! YOU'RE HITTING THAT SPOT! OH YES BABY! ON SHIT! FUCK ME! OH FUCK! FUCK! OH YEAH! I'M CUMMING ALL OVER THAT DICK BABY! OH YES JULHO! FUCK ME!" she cried out at the top of her lungs as we chilled out in the Jacuzzi in my hotel suite as I gave her my huge massive rock hard cock.

She had her legs wrapped around my waist as I pinned her against the side of the pool while I nibbled and bit all over neck while I was making her scream my name at the top of her lungs.

I was fucking her brains out while I felt my balls smacked up against her asshole whole I felt her drag her nails down my back.

I was kissing all over her neck while I leaned down to suck on her hard nipples as she screamed my nail while I felt her tensed up for me as I looked down and watched my cream coated cock slide in and out of her while she screamed my name as I could not keep my hands off of her.

The jets from the pool coated our electric bodies to the point I was surprised that we didn't get electrocuted. The heat between us was so intense that we could have burned Satan because we were so intense that we could have exploded. I could not stop pushing her button and she was fucking me like she was never going to get this dick ever again.

"Oh shit Julho! Oh yeah baby! I'm cumming again! Oh fuck baby! Oh my fucking God baby! Oh yes! Yes! Yes! Oh yes baby!" she cried out in pain as I watched her body go limp while I kept pounding it deep inside of her.

I had both of my hands on that massive ass of hers while I kept pounding the life out of her. I picked her up out of the Jacuzzi and pinned her against the wall of my high dollar suite as I pounding the life out of her.

She was laying her neck back against the white beans in my ultra-luxury hotel room as she ran her hands down my shoulders while I worked it deep in her while I gave her the dick that she refused to turn her loose as her pussy lips gripped the life out of my shaft before I pulled out almost all the way before I shoved it back deep inside of her to make her squirm in pleasure.

I looked deep into her green eyes as I felt the intensity grow between us. I could feel what started out as small sparks between us grow into a full out flame thrower that morphed into an erupting volcano that erupted with passion between us as the smoke grew and nothing could cool us odd because the connection between us was so magical that nothing could stop us until we both got ours.

As she wrapped her arms around my neck, the Brazilian freak showed off her flexibility as she wrestled her ankles on my shoulders while I kept pounding the fuck out of her. I pulled out just about all the way as I fucked her tight pussy with just my head for a few seconds before I pushed my way all the way deep inside of her a couple of times as my foot long cock was dripped and the lustful recoil from inside of her made me tense up a little bit as her huge bubble butt refused to stop bouncing freely as I ran my hands over her silhouette and kissed her passionately before I felt myself starting to tense up inside of her.

I kicked into fifth gear as I got ready to blow my sexual transmission as I held her close to me and fucked her like a jackrabbit. She tensed up and held me close to her while I felt her racing heartbeat match the rhythm of mine. I grabbed that fat ass and refused to turn her loose as I she cried out for me while I filled up the inside of her with five loads of cum deep inside of her before she collapsed in my arms as I held her close to me and refused to let her go.

'So when can you move in?" I asked.

'I already told my manager that this is going to be my last week here." She told me before she kissed me on the lips and I ran my hands on her sweaty curvy body before I started to regain my composure while I felt her small hands run over my body before I kissed her passionately and got ready for my first of several Abu Dhabi match-up tomorrow afternoon.

First Part of the Dream

I made the two hour drive with Professor Nogueria in my blacked out 2008 Chevrolet Avalanche on 24 inch rims to the Storm Arena that was hosting this years Abu Dhabi Combat Championship tournament on Riverside Beach, Loira de Areia, Brazil.

I stepped out with my duffle bag and flip flops as Professor Nogueria held my bag and I took a couple of sips of water while I headed inside of the building. Since I was one of the competitors, they were taking pictures of all of us as we walked inside.

I looked at the time and saw that my first match started in a couple of hours. I had found a couple of the officials before I got weighed in and saw that I had come in at just under a hundred and sixty-one pounds which I admit was pretty impressive considering the fact I'm doing a one hundred and eighty-five pound tournament next month.

***

As the tournament went on, I saw that it was getting close to the time for my first match-up of the evening. Since I was recently promoted to a first degree black belt in Brazilian Jiu-Jitsu, I wanted a step up in competition, and I believe that I was going to get that in the form of one opponent that I was a little nervous about going up against. I was referring to none other than nothing lower than a 3rd degree black belt and some of the most elite grapplers in the world.

I might be a professional mixed martial artist and the best grappler in all of mixed martial arts, but now I was going up against some people that only did Brazilian Jiu-Jitsu or Judo for a living.

The upside of this whole tournament was that it was all no-gi so I had that to work in my favor. I had brought along five different walkout shirts because I was thinking positive that I was going to win my weight bracket, the Openweight, and the Absolute division because I was not only known for my drive, but my stubbornness and maybe over confident in myself.

I walked over to the locker rooms and got ready for my final preparations before it was time for my match-ups. I had to do my final rituals and clear my head before I got ready to knock the dust off both of my black belts and show them why The Cobra was just as legal on the mats as I am inside of an eight sided octagon.

Second Part of the Dream

It was finally time for me to get the show on the road from my standpoint. I was wearing a super tight black rash guard along with a pair of matching black shorts with a cobra wrapped around the right leg along with a black ankle bracelet to show that I was going to be in the back corner.

It was pretty cool that I was used as an alternate a few people got injured so I was already in the finals already. I had already prequalified and I was going to be fighting for my first ADCC World Championship and I was ready

I found out my very first opponent was going to be none other than Ted Vieira. Ted was from Sao Paulo, Brazil and was one very scary grappler. He might be only 5'9, but his guard and guillotines were nothing to play with. He was a 4th degree black belt and a former two time ADCC champion so there was no way that I could deny his credit. He might not look intimidating, but his twenty-six wins and three losses as a grappling record, with twenty-three of them by the way of submission. He had twenty of them by the way of guillotine that means he does not play around on the mats and I was ready to go up against him.

The referee motioned for us to come to the center of the mats as the bald headed light skinned legendary grappler came to the mat in his tight fitting dark blue compression shorts. He adjusted them one last time before he made sure his sleeves on his white rash guard were just so as we stepped onto the mats together at the same time. After we shook hands, the referee motioned for us to start our match-up.

Without wasting a second, Ted quickly shot in and attempted to take me down to the mat with a double leg takedown. I sprawled out of the situation and hook my arm under his before I leaped over him and took him to the ground with a modified hip toss that threw him off balance for the moment. He tried to posture up as I laid down on my back and pulled him by his wrist as I pulled him deep inside of closed guard. The crowd was cheering the whole time as I released the grip on his arm as I let the kimura attempt go before I wrapped my arm around his neck and went for a guillotine of my own. I grabbed my wrist and bent his neck downwards as I leaned to the side while the crowd began cheering while ted tried to find his way out of the submission. It wasn't long before I felt him tap a couple of times before so that I could be the new ADCC +66 kg weight Class Champion.

As I came to the awards ceremony, I had the championship belt placed around my waist and the medal put around my neck. A couple of that came in behind me to win the silver and bronze medals which was a warm filling. Diamonds might be a woman's best friend, but gold is this champion's best friend.

Third Part of the Dream

Since I had won my first ADCC victory by submission with a deep guillotine, I had advanced to the Openweight Championship part of the tournament in my weight bracket. I was slightly more nervous about my next opponent who happened to be someone who was a little more deadly than Ted Vieira. I was going up against Charles Kyle.

Charles Kyle was a second degree black belt in Brazilian Jiu-Jitsu along with being a former collegiate wrestler from Tampa Bay, Florida. He won a silver medal in the Olympics in collegiate wrestling after taking out some of the toughest people on the planet. He was a submission wrestler that held a grappling record of thirty-two wins and five losses with twenty-eight of them by the way of submission. He was slightly intimidating because of the fact that he was biggest man in the competition. He stood right at six feet, five inches tall and weighed in at two hundred and forty five pounds. This was not his first time doing this since he was a former heavyweight champion in the ADCC. He was no means a small man to be looked passed, but at the same time, I was no slouch either.

I came to the mats wearing a different pair of black shorts a black tribal printed tee-shirt. As I stepped onto the mat and got ready for my match-up, I looked at the dark headed former Marine who was looking down on me with a slight smirk on his face. He adjusted his gray shorts and rain his head over his bald headed as he stepped onto the mat before the referee motioned for us to shake hands and start the match-up.

As he quickly grabbed my left wrist, I squatted down and hooked his right leg before I shot in to take him down to the mat before he used his weight advantage and trapped me in his closed guard. I saw that he still had my left wrist and tried to switch his hips before he tried to lean to the side and get me in an armbar attempt. I quickly rolled away from him before while I pushed up and pulled my arm free as I pounced onto his back and secured the first two hooks of the rear naked choke as I locked both of my tree trunk like legs around his waist to control the bigger man. As he laid back and tried to throw me, I hung on until he tried to grab ahold of one of my wrist. Before I knew it, I had capitalized on the mistake that he had made before I threw my arm around his throat and started squeezing in attempt to choke him out with one arm. He used both of his arms to free my arm, but it didn't work because I wiggled my arm free and clamped the choke deep on him as he held onto for as long as he could. I hyperextended as far back as I could and final Goliath gave in and tapped against my wrist before I won my second straight victory and my second ADCC championship.

As I stood to my feet, I was presented with my second championship belt for the night along with another medal. I was more than overjoyed as I raised both of my arms as I celebrated before I left the mats and got ready to head to the locker room so that I could get prepped for my third match-up to see if I could keep the momentum going.

A Shock of the Night

I was outside taking a quick breather while the women were grappling inside and I needed some fresh air. I had been inside of the arena full of fifteen thousand people and I needed my alone time. I might be a celebrity, but I had no problem saying that I was an introvert that valued my own time away from the public eye.

As I stepped on the glass steps on the outside of the arena and watched the cars drive by, I pulled out my phone and saw that I had missed a phone call from my wife. I quickly called her back since she had not been as big of a pain lately and I was curious about what she might have had to say. I saw that there was a voice message that had been left and I could only imagine what she was telling me.

After I went through the steps to retrieve my voice message, I waited patiently to hear what was about to go down.

"The following message is from Melanie Berry-Damm." The dispatcher replied as I got ready to hear what she was about to say.

'Hey honey. I know that we haven't been talking as much lately, but you have no idea how much. I miss you. It's hard rolling over at night not being in your arms. I love you so much and I'm so horny right now. I wish that foot long black dick was so deep inside of me right now. I wish that you had my knees pinned to my chest while you had your hand on my throat and fucked me like the bitch that I've been lately. I want you to fuck me until I cum and scream your name at the top of my lungs. Baby, I'm running my hands over this smooth hairy pussy while I stick a couple of fingers deep inside and tease my clit. When I get to Brazil, I want you to manhandle me. I want you to make me your sex slave. I want you make me wish that you had never left me in the first place. Nothing is off limits and I want to be your fucking whore! I'm about to head to Brazil and my plane touches down Monday at two thirty in Loira de Areia Airport. I'll see you then. I love you baby. Mwah!" she exclaimed before she hung up.

I was in another gear. She must have been feeling some kind of way and I'm going to make her want me as soon as she gets back in my hometown.

The Hunger to be the Best

I had entered my first ADCC tournament and I had already became a two time champion. I had a new outlook within this tournament along with my mixed martial arts career. On the day that retire from doing mixed martial arts, I am going to become a full time grappler and probably hold seminars across the globe along with just doing grappling submission tournaments like these.

I had my wife acting like she was in somewhat in a good mood. She might have just been acting happy because she was about to go on vacation for her first time out of the country. I had already paid for everything depise the fact she made around forty grand a year and had another seventy stacks in the bank because she saved all the allowances I had given her. *She must have been playing something unless she was just that stingy.*

I was looking forward to seeing Yolanda today. She had texted me and told me that she had surprise for me back at home since she had slowly started moving in and almost had everything taken care of. She even had her own spot to crash perfectly to the point that it made the most luxurious hotel room look like a roach motel. From the way she treated me at the hotel, I can only imagine how she is going to treat me when I get back home.

I was looking forward to getting this match over and done with since I was becoming one of the most decorated martial artist of all time at a young age which was a warm feeling. I had never felt what it felt like to have a knockout my career of wins. *Maybe one day I will get to that point, but for the time being, I had to focus on winning the ADCC Absolute Division title that I was going to break through the glass ceiling and bring home with me, even if I had to bring my opponent's arm along with me for the ride.*

I went inside of the arena wearing a pair of black and white shorts with a sketched cobra on the legs and the Cobra's face on my backside with a matching tee-shirt that had my name on the back of it. I had readjusted my ponytail and go to up against my opponent who was the two time +88 Division ADCC Champion who boasted an undefeated 7-0 record in the ADCC tournament and I was looking forward to going up against none other than Jackson McKinney.

As I stepped onto the mats against the stocky, five foot six country boy who boasted a fifth degree black belt in Brazilian Jiu-Jitsu along with one of the best Brazilian Jiu-Jitsu schools in all of Texas. He ran his hands over his spiky blonde hair and adjusted his white tee-shirt with his light blue fight shorts. *Honestly he reminded me of a bigger version of Sean Sherk.*

As we both stepped onto the mats, we shook hands because we had the most respect for each other. We were both undefeated grapplers that had won championship gold tonight and planned on adding to the collection that we was taking home.

As the referee called to start the match-up, we both shot in on each other. He was a stronger dude but anyone who had any kind of experience with Brazilian Jiu-Jitsu will tell you that strength is not all that matters, when each match is really a giant chess match and the ultimate victory is choking the king out with a creative submission.

As we went to the mat and rolled around for the spectators while we tried our hardest to get the submission on each other. I felt him sit up as he grabbed my leg and went for a leg lock of some sort that happened to be his speciality along with the rear naked choke. I rolled away from it as I wrapped my legs around his waist with the closed guard as he tried his best to posture up to get better positioning. He stood to his feet before he tried to fight me off and attempt to take me down and get me in full mount to he could use his weight and size against me. I was not for trying to get into that kind of a predicament so I went ahead and let the guard go as I laid on my back and hooked my leg around his and went for a De La Riva guard and held onto his foot. He tried to fight it off as he leaped forward only for me to lock his foot down and get him in a heel hook of my own before I got it in deep and tried my best to finish him. His leg literally looked like a tree trunk as I torqued back on his ankle before I watched him tap on the mat a couple of times before I ended his undefeated streak and won my third championship all in one day.

As I was given my third championship belt from the Absolute Division of the ADCC tournament. I had the championship placed around my waist as Professor Nogueria placed the other two championship belts around my shoulders. I had three of my medals placed around my neck as one of the news reporters walked up to me to hear my words on the fight.

"Julho, you have just entered your your first Abu Dhabi Combat Championship tournament and won your third championship belt within a matter of minutes. You have taken down some serious heavyweights in the history of the tournament. You have choked out Ted Vieira and submitted Jackson McKinney. You are the +66 Champion, Absolute Champion, and OpenWeight Champion. So what is your opinion in the way that this tournament went?" she asked.

"I mean this is not an easy competition. These were so heavy hitters that I have looked up to when I first started out doing grappling. I was working as hard as I could to train for this competition to work in this competition. When I first got the invite to be in the competition, I was more than happy. I refused to get eliminated and I wanted to put on a good show. Being a former Brazilian Jiu-Jitsu World Champion and recently getting my First degree black belt in Brazilian Jiu-Jitsu, I wanted to prove that this is the kind of place that I belonged and I wanted to show everyone that I am going to be the best." I replied before I left the building with Professor Nogueria.

Championship Tournament

Today had been a good day and I was about to have a good night. I had just dropped off Professor Nogueria back at his house across the street before I backed up in my driveway beside my new Ferrari F-430 Spyder and grabbed all of my championship belts and medals as I headed inside before I went inside of my house and headed upstairs to find my championship trophy case and placed all three of my new championships beside my other MMA championships and medals that I had won over the course of my life. I was now a three time ADCC Champion and no one could take that honor away from me.

I locked them away in the case as I took off my walkout tee and tossed it into the laundry along with the rest of my clothes for her to clean later on. I was glad that I didn't have to these kinds of things, so I had someone else to do it for me.

The way was still early and looked at the horizon at the beach. I let my hair down that I was going to get braided soon. I looked over my clean slate of a chiseled frame and thought about adding some ink later on. I felt like I was on top of the word and wanted to share it with the one that I truly loved, but the one that I loved seemed like she wanted to be in a part time marriage. *Maybe I should have waited before I offically said I do.*

"Is the Cobra here?" she asked in a sexy voice.

"Yeah baby," I replied in a lightly depressed tone before I came back to reality as I started to look around and saw my lovely mistress and new maid standing there dressing up like a cheap two dollar hooker.

She had on a super short denim skirt that barely covered her ass with her huge ass and thighs hanging out that was lightly coated with her black fishhet stockings. She was looking good with all off her delicious curves hanging out as her cutt off midriff with her perky breast standing at attention of me. She looked like a cheap two dollar hoe along the cheap two dollar make-up that made me want want to just give her a five dollar blowjob and throw in an extra ten bucks to get some action.

"Hey papi," she replied in a playful tone before she ran her hands over my muscular frame as I pulled her close to me.

"Remember that there is no kissing. That's intimacy. I only share that with my lover." she replied as she played the slutty part of the act while she took me by the hand and headed downstairs and outside to the backyard. We walked around to the back of the house as she pinned me up against the giant oak tree in the middle of yard as I looked ahead at the beach side view.

I felt her reach for the bulge in my fight shorts while she jumped back on her knees instinctively. She undid my drawstrings before she snatched them down around my knees before my rock hard cock jumped at attention for her. She playfully teased my head before she ran her tongue up both sides of my shaft as I felt my swollen head venture inside of her mouth. She started to get deeper on me with each time she bobbed up and down on me. She was giving me the sloppiest head and my trick for the eating was treating me like she had no emotional connection to me. I was having my head teased miserably as she looked up at me with those seductive green bedroom eyes while I was enjoying the pleasure that she was giving to me. I felt as she gave me a supertight seal as she literally sucked the black of me as I enjoyed every second of pleasure that she was giving to me. I could feel my head singing in pleasure as I held her around the back of the head while she refused to give me a second to breathe. I could feel her tonsils massaging the tip of my head as she pulled her mouth off of me while I she went to sucking my balls. Her tongue was so gentle and yet so forceful that if she was a real hooker, she would but some of the most sophiscated escorts out of business.

She didn't say a words as she stood to her feet and bent over to show me the goods under her skirt. She wasn't wearing any kind of underwear and I felt her starting to back it up for me before she grabbed me just below the head and looked around like she was looking out for cops trying to bust her for prostitution even if she was just roleplaying.

I felt myself entering her deep from behind as I watched her spread her legs while she welcomed me inside. I grabbed her wide hips and started pounding her hard from the back while felt her smooth lips kiss my head as I went deep inside of my hoe for the night. She grabbed my balls and massaged them as I pounded away deep inside of her as I refused to ease up on her. She closed her eyes as she rested her other hand against the cold bark of the tree while she begged out for mercy as all 12 inches of me slid in and out of her virgin tightess. I watched as she looked over her shoulder and I grabbed her around the back of the head before she looked back at me as I leaned all of my force inside of her while she was moaning for me before I came up behind her and hugged her close to me from behind. I stroked her silhouette as I massaged her lower back before I ran my hands over that huge ass of hers and spanked her a couple of times while she moaned out in pleasure. I made her beg for more while I was listening to her moan something sensual.

"Oh shit baby! Fuck me right there baby! Oh shit baby! Oh yes baby! FFFUUUUCCKK!" she cried out as I spanked her a few times as I used all of my upper body strength and hit her with some hard pelvic thrust from the back while I was still pounding away at her like a mad man.

"Hurry up baby!" she cried as she acted as if she had to move onto her next trick. I started to pick up the pace as if I was trying to get on and move on about my business while I worked it in her to her delight. I felt myself thickening inside of her before I pounded her a couple of more times before I held her close to me and fired a couple of huge loads of cum deep inside of her as she walked off bowlegged as I looked at her with a light smirk before we walked inside of the massive estate together.

"Julho, how did you like being my jon for a little while?" she teased as I spanked her huge ass a couple of times before we walked up to my bedroom together.

"It was great, but I have something to tell you." I told her since I was a straight shooter.

"Okay, what's up?" she asked.

"My wife is coming in for vacation on Monday. She is going to be here for a couple of weeks and there is a chance she might be moving here so act normal." I told her.

"Okay, no problem." she assured me as she kissed me on the lips and I watched her huge ass sashay from left to right as she walked out of my bedroom and headed on her way to proceed with whatever chores that needed to be done.

The Return of My First Love

I was waiting at the airport in my massive pick-up that I had just gotten lifted a little bit and added some new 33 inch off road tires to make it my own. My wife would be out shortly and I still hadn't told her about my new live in maid. She probably figured out that I was cheating on her, and something in my stomach told me that she was cheating on me, but I wanted to make this marriage work.

I looked down at my ring finger and saw my wedding ring that I had worn for the first time in a while. I thought about how things were flowing so well that if we were still happy when we were when we had first gotten married, we would have renewed our wedding vows, but things are slowly starting to change for the worst.

Since she was flying out to see me, I was going to try my best to be on my best behavior. I know that I had to have been cheated on with someone, but I had no idea who it was, but hey, we have to get ours.

I was scared to death of what she might say. It was getting close to three and I was sweating bullets. I had not seen her since I first left the United States, but we still stayed in contact. I was curious about how this would go.

Since I was in the truck today, I had enough room for all of my wife's excess baggage that she was always break down. I was waiting patiently as I looked around to see if I could see if I find the one that I had given my heart to only for her to mistreat me whenever I was fighting. I was never had seen her at any of my fights unless I begged her to come see me fight and now I'm going to worry her about coming to at least one of my fights since she was never supportive of anything that I did outside of the octagon.

"Julho!" I heard a loud familiar voice scream before I turned around to see my wife coming my direction wearing nothing but a pink dress that barely came past her mid tight. She was dressed more open minded as she came to me with her hair in a small ponytail and a huge smile on her face. I was so happy to see her as she ran up to me and gave me a giant hug and kissed me on the lips before I kissed her passionately. I ran my hands over her slender frame while I held her close to me and I felt her drawing me close to me and I didn't want to turn her loose.

"Baby, I missed you so much!" I told her truthfully as I looked down at her and saw a tear flow down her face while I watched her face buried in my muscular chest while I was enjoying my time with her.

"I missed you too baby." I replied as the assistant at the airport loaded her luggage into the back of the truck while I froze in time being with my wife.

I walked up her to the passenger's side door and she hopped in as I got a glimpse of her hairy bush that she refused to shave. *The girl could literally be a cavewoman if she wanted to be without struggling.*

I slipped the assistant a hundred dollar bill for making job a little less stressful for me. He took a couple of pictures with me since I was a bit of a high profile celebrity in the area.

I started the engine to the truck as the sound of some hard rock thumped from the speakers. I threw on my Sao Paulo F.C. fitted hat and headed back to the house so that she could get settled in because I had something special planned for her.

Undefeated Undisputed XFA Middleweight Championship of the World

I was backstage with Professor Nogueria, his two sons, and his daughter who were all holding my champion belts. I was on top of the world, and I was determined to leave the building a four time champion. I know that this is going to be my last fight with all of them here. We rolled around the school and they helped me tighten up my game and I felt like I was ready for him.

As the sound of "Headstrong" by Trapt came from the speakers, I came out onstage with my crew. We were all surrounded by security as I came to the end of the stage, and twenty explosions went off before I walked down the ramp and shook hands with everyone. As I reached the cage, I took off my walkout tee and hat and handed it off to Professor Nogueria. I looked into the crowd to see the owner of the NFC in the audience to watch the fight. I felt the Vaseline get applied to my face, while the referee checked my gloves. I got the okay as I hugged all of my camp before I put in my mouth guard before I headed to my neutral corner and got ready for my match-up.

As the arena went pitch black, the crowd started screaming. The the sound of "Oh Let's Do It" by Waka Flocka Flame as the flames came from the stage. As the taller black man came down the ramp with both of his championship belts around his waist. He shook hands with the fans as he reached the cage. He stripped down to his fight shorts and handed his championship belt off before they threw the Vaseline on his face. The referee okay him as he put his mouth guard in and came into the cage and looked down at me a little bit as we got ready to hear the introductions.

"The following match is scheduled for five, five minute rounds and it's for the XFA Undisputed Middleweight Championship of the World!" exclaimed the ring announcer as the crowd started cheering.

"In the blue corner from Loira de Areia, Brazil! He stands at six feet, one inch tall and weighed in at one hundred and eight three pounds! He has a fighting background in Judo and Brazilian Jiu-Jitsu where he has black belts in both disciplines. He holds a professional record of twenty-one wins and zero losses with all twenty-one of them finishing in the first round. He is the XFA Lightweight Grand Prix Champion, the XFA Middleweight Grand Prix tournament Champion and the current, reigning, and defending XFA Welterweight Champion. Give it up for Julho "The Cobra" Damm!" exclaimed the ring announcer as the crowd cheered for me.

"And in the red corner from Detroit, Michigan in the white shorts! He stands at six feet, three inches tall and weighed in at one hundred and eighty-five pounds! He has a fighting background in Muay Thai, Judo, and Brazilian Jiu-Jitsu where he is a black belt. He holds a perfect professional record of twenty-three wins and zero losses with twelve by knockout and eleven by submission. He is the XFA Interim Light Heavyweight Champion, and the current, reigning, and defending XFA Middleweight Champion. He is none other than Justine Sanders!" as the referee motioned for both of us to come to the center of the cage.

"I want a clean fight. Follow my rules at all times and remember this is for the belt. Punch gloves and let's do this!" Replied the referee as we shook our heads and went back to our neutral corners and as the referee called for the bell to start the match.

The crowd came out of their seats as we got ready to cage each other. He tried to use his Muay Thai skills as he went for a high knee on me. I took the body shot and kicked him in the side with a body shot that he took. He was a skilled grappler and I didn't underestimate him as I wrapped my arms around his waist and before I got a chance to tackle him, the bigger champion tackled me to the ground before I got a chance to mount an offense. As I hit the ground, I held his wrist and pulled him close to me and deep into my open guard before I threw my leg over his shoulder and secured the Rubber Guard as I controlled the bigger champion. It was a position that a lot of people didn't see often. I watched as he tried to pass the guard before I leaned and followed him as I threw punches to his face to nullify his striking ability. I thought about spinning out of it and get him flat on his stomach so that I could put him in an omoplata, but I have seen him get out of that position numerous times in grappling tournaments. I tagged him a couple of times with some hard punches of my own as I secured my leg under his chin and pulled down on the back of his head with a Muay Thai clinch to secure the gogoplata submission hold that no one had ever passed. I laid down on the ground before I got him to tap out to end his undefeated streak and win my fourth championship belt with the promotion.

My training camp came into the championship belt with all of my championships that I had previously won. I hugged my camp and put on my hat and walkout tee before I came to the center of the ring to hear the results of the match-up.

"The winner of this match, going into the first round at one minute and forty-five seconds by the way of gogoplata tapout submission and the new XFA Undisputed Middleweight Champion of the World! Julho "The Cobra" Damm!" exclaimed the ring announcer as the crowd gave me a roaring ovation as my fourth championship belt was placed around my waist.

"Julho, you have just won your fourth title by submission. You have dominated and ended Justine Saunders championship reign by gogoplata. What is your words on this fight?" The ring announcer asked.

"Well honestly I knew I had my work out for me. He was a stand up striker as well as a grappler. I wanted to pick apart his game and make him go into unfamiliar territory. I made him tap and my fourth title feels amazing." I replied as I left the cage with a little more gold to add to my collection.

Assume the Position

As soon as I said my final good-byes to Professor Nogueria's family, I dropped them all off at the airport before I headed back to my house. I grabbed my championship belts from inside the pick-up truck and locked my pick-up behind me as I came inside of my house.

I locked the door behind me and tossed my keys into the candy dish as I went upstairs and placed the Lightweight Grand Prix and Middleweight Grand Prix Championship belts inside of the trophy cabinet before I locked it and went to the downstairs bedroom to find my mistress who was downstairs and inside of her bedroom as she looked like she was waiting for me.

"Hey you bad criminal." She replied playfully as I closed the door behind me and looked at her wearing the sexy policewoman's uniform with everything on display. I looked at her ass hanging out of the uniform as I walked up behind her and spanked her a couple of times as I kissed her on the neck and she reached back and massaged my bulge while I got ready to give her pussy what for.

"I heard that you have been a very bad boy. I want you to assume the position so that I can deal with you." She told me as she took her huge ass and pinned me against the wall and grinded up against me while I ran my hands over her curvy body as she moaned in pleasure.

I slowly found myself sitting in a corner before she smothered me with that huge bunda of hers as I enjoyed the facial that I was receiving from her. I laid back and enjoyed the pleasure before she snatched her thong to the side and forced my nose up her asshole while I tongued her pussy long and hard from behind. I watched as she reached down and touched her toes as she gyrated seductively against my face while I enjoyed the lustful facial that she wanted to give me. I was trying my best to keep my composure as I sucked on the fat pussy lips and started to tongue her asshole in unison. I could not stop myself from giving the sexy cop her rights as I read her rights to her with my tongue and forced her to submit to my own law. I was making her tense up as she rested one of her arms against the wall for balance before she started shivering in pleasure to the point that she couldn't take any more of my tongue.

"Give me that dick!" she moaned for me as I leaned back and she grabbed me just above the base of my foot long piece of sausage as I sat down in the recliner before she massaged my shaft with her lips for a couple of minutes before she squatted down on my huge cock and started bouncing up and down on me.

She was trying her best to keep quiet as I snatched her uniform open as she leaned back while I sucked on her nipples. I was giving her Brazilian officer my foot long baton as I administered my law on her.

She was rubbing her fingers of her clit while I looked deep into her green eyes while she squirmed in pleasure to the point that she started shivering and having mini convulsions while I was trying my best to make sure that she was keeping quiet while I gave her my form of police brutality. She rested her feet on my thighs and bounced on me in the fastest moves as she took the authority from me and fucked the life out of me until I felt myself getting ready to blow my load since I had just gotten out of a fight before I had gotten out here.

I spanked her a couple of times before she stood to her feet and bend over for me as I watched her spread her legs seductively before she smacked her fat clit. I stroked myself a couple of times before I pushed my head deep inside of her as she let out a light moan before I grabbed her around the back of the neck brutalized the officer as I tried to get charged with a life sentence for abusing and beating the officer's walls with my massive nightstick to the point that she couldn't take it. I was using all of my force deep inside of her while she dropped her head in pleasure as I refused to slow down on her. She looked over her shoulder at me while my cock started to grow inside of her before I pushed out almost all the way and fucked her with my huge head before I shoved it all the way until I hit something special and made her cum for me as I unloaded inside of her and she collapsed on the bed beside me.

"Julho, that felt so good." She moaned before she kissed me like she didn't want me to leave her.

'That was great. I have to get upstairs before Melanie suspects anything. You know how crazy my wife is." I told her after I kissed her passionately grabbed my championship belts and went upstairs so that I could try to hide my recent altercation with my maid even if she did already know about it.

Sixth Title Defense

I had to get my mind off the fact that I was back on the outs with my wife despite the fact that I was still sleeping with my maid. I know that does not make things better, but it helps to ease the pain that I have been having to face on a daily basis.

This was the last fight on my contract, and I wanted to out with a bang. I had given my heart and soul to this promotion in return for some of the best fans and more money than I could ever dream of spending. I was ready to show the number one contender what happens when you mess with 'The Cobra.'

As I walked down the hallway of the backstage area, I listened to the words of wisdom from Professor Nogueria. I had been training my ass off to win this fight and I was not going to let all this hard work seem like a waste. I had been working on my cardio since it seemed as if I was starting to gas a little bit in the ADCC tournament which I know was something that I had been needing to work on. I was not shy about what I thought of my opponent and as I stepped through the curtains, I knew that it was game time.

The sound of "The Blister Still Exist" by Slipknot jumped through the speakers as the crowd came to life. I came out with Professor

Nogueria who was holding all of the championship belts I had won with the promotion to delight of the fans. I raised both of my arms and six explosions went off as I walked down the ramp and shook hands with the fans before I looked to my left and saw my wife and as I looked to my right and saw my mistress wearing one of my walkout tees to my delight. As soon as I reached the cage, I took off my walkout tee and my hat and handed it off to Professor Nogueria. The referee checked my gloves as Vaseline was applied to my face and I got the okay as I hugged my trainer and put in my mouthguard before I went to my neutral corner.

I looked up at my opponent who they called the number one contender. I looked up and down at the five foot nine scrawny little wannabe who had a little temple fade and some fake gangster tattoos all over him. He thought that he was all that since he was the one who had one knockout along with more descisions than I could count.

"The following match is the main event and its scheduled for five, five minute rounds and it's for the XFA Welterweight Championship!" exclaimed the announcer as the crowd started to die down.

"In the blue corner from Kingston, Jamacia in the white and red shorts. He stands at five feet, nine inches tall and weighed in at one hundred and seventy pounds. He holds a fighting background in Boxing, Hapkido, and Tae Kwon Do where he is a black belt. He holds a professional record of nineteen wins and six losses with two of them by the way of knockout and seventeeen of them by the way of desicicion. He is none other than Lloyd Makins!" exclaimed the ring announcer as the crowd started booing him.

"And in the red corner from Loira de Areia, Brazil! He stands at six feet, one inch tall and weighed in at one hundred and sixty-nine pounds! He has a fighting background in Judo and Brazilian Jiu-Jitsu where he has black belts in both disciplines. He holds a professional record of twenty-seven wins and zero losses with all twenty-seven of them finishing in the first round. He is the XFA Lightweight Grand Prix Champion, The XFA Middleweight Grand Prix Champion, The XFA Middleweight Champion, and the current, reigning, and defending XFA Welterweight Champion going into his sixth title defense. Give it up for Julho"The Cobra" Damm!" exclaimed the ring announcer as the referee motioned for both of us to come to the center of the cage.

"I went over the rules with both of you in your locker rooms. I want a clean fight and punch gloves if you would like to. Remember this is for the belt." he replied as we both shook our heads and went back to our neutral corners.

As the referee called for the bell, we both charged each other as he tried to knock my head off. I ducked all of his strikes as I shot in and wrapped my arms around his waist and took him to the ground with a suplex that looked like something from a wrestling match. I watched as he tried to fight me off from his back as I watched him try to throw an elbow from the back. I looked over my shoulder as I stood to my feet and lifted him off the ground again before I released the suplex and wrapped my legs around his waist. I went for a rear naked choke attempt, but he defended it and held onto my wrist while I laid on my back and and watched him fall prey to my open guard. He broke one of his wrist free from my clutches and I used both of my arms and pulled him close to me before I wrapped both of my legs around his shoulder and around his neck to keep him at bay with my triangle choke. He tried his best to free himself by wiggling free, but failed miserably, I didn't even get a bruise on me as I pulled back on his arm with an armbar submission to add to the deep triangle choke. I kept my composure as I leaned to the side and added torque to the shoulder joint as I used all of my strength to lock down the submission to make him tap out to give me my twenty-eight straight victory.

As I released the submission, I looked into the crowd to see Yolanda rush into the cage with Master Nogueria to hug me before I looked over at Melanie who was giving the sarcastic clap before the referee motioned for me to come to the center of the cage. *It's amazing how some people can be so ungrateful for all the good things you do to them.*

The winner of this match going into the first round at one minute and thirty-nine seconds by the way of tapout choke submission and still champion, Julho 'The Cobra' Damm!" exclaimed the ring announcer as my new championship belt was placed around my waist as the announcer walked up to me.

"Julho, you have made history! You have defended your belt a total of six times along with the other championship belts to add to your resume. You have just ended Makins streak of terror so what's your opinion of this fight?" He asked.

"Well he was a crafty fighter that does not give up. Winning this fight was a warm feeling and it feels good to know that I have fufilled my contract on a high note and still the champion." I replied as I left the cage and headed off on my way to see what was next for me.

One for the Road

"Oh shit baby! You're fucking the shit out of me! Your dick is hitting my spot baby! Oh yes baby! Oh shit baby! Fuck me! Oh my fucking yes! Oh yeah! Fuck!" she cried out as I pinned her knees to her chest while I was pounding the shit out of her. She had her legs spread for me while I laid deep inside of her with each thrust as I made her scream my name at the tip of her lungs.

She was in a spread-eagle position as held onto her wrist while I squatted down on her as I got deeper inside of her with each thrust.

After the way that she snapped on me, I grabbed her around the throat while I she gasped for air to take out my frustration on my estranged wife.

She was starting to slightly choke as she gasped for air and I looked deep into her hazel eyes. She was begging for mercy as tears started to flow down her face as my dick massaged her love tunnel while she was arched her back to take me even deeper inside of her. I fucked her harder and deeper as the meat on her bones jiggled in pleasure to the stroke of each one of my thrust to the point that I was making her wish that she had never pissed me off. The fuel in my eyes kicked me into another gear while I was definitely bruising something inside of her. I would not be surprised if I had punctured her uterus as she held her stomach in pain while the tears flowed down her face.

I felt myself getting close to my point as I turned her throat loose as she catch her breath and I picked her hips off the ground as I fucked her as hard and deep as I could until I shot a huge geyser of pleasure deep inside of her before she moaned in pleasure as I pulled out and kissed her on the lips.

"That was wonderful?" she replied as she looked up at me with a smile before she sat up and kissed me on the lips and held me close to her before I got ready to cuddled up with her and snuggle up alongside her before she fell asleep in the sheets beside me.

Walk Away

I was a bit of a free agent within the promotion. I had fought all of the fights on the contract and I still had all the championship belts. I was going to take some time off before I signed my new contract, but at the same time I wanted to let my body rest so that I could do some other things that I had been wanting to do with my wife.

I wanted to try out motorcycle racing. I wanted to try out modeling. I wanted to try out acting a little bit. I wanted to spend some time with some of my loved ones. I wanted to try to work on my marriage and have a family of my own since I didn't have one coming up.

As soon as I got back to my house from training with Professor Nogueria, I cut the engine to my truck before I dashed inside and went upstairs to my bedroom so that I could try and talk to my wife. It was too quiet because I know that Yolanda had class today and Melanie never left the house. As soon as I got to my room, I went upstairs and found a letter on the nightstand with my name on it. *I know that this had to be good.*

'Dear Julho

I have been with you for the past few years. We have been married for three years and we have been together for the past five years. I have

given you my heart and we have been together through thick and thin. I

had given all that I have only for you to cheat on me. I took a vacation

so that I could be with you only for you to cheat on me with the maid. I

know that she is a good person, but she might be better for you than me.

I want to live my life without the idea of someone cheating on me. The

thought of being with you for the rest of my life sounds like pure hell.

You live your life. My flight departs at twelve thirty. I'll see you another

time. Have a nice life.

It was nice knowing you,

Love you always,

Melanie'

After reading that letter, I dashed downstairs and left in the Ferrari

as I headed to the airport like a madman. Fuck the speed limits because

love doesn't have a speed. I had tried my hardest to savage this marriage

despite the fact that her family and friends hated me with a passion. I

thought about all of the arguments and the times we had spent together. I

remember the times when she told me wanted to have children, but she

didn't think that she could have any. She talked about how much she had

loved the idea of adopting and I was ready. I told her that I wanted to

have three children regardless if they were biological or not as long as they were with the one that I loved.

I was on the interstate and I looked the streets and made the usual fifteen minute drive in roughly three minutes as I pulled into the parking lot and pulled up to see if I could see her anywhere.

"Julho!" I heard a loud voice scream as I turned around to see my wife standing there as she waved at me from the plane before she blew me a kiss and loaded onto the plane. As I watched the plane load and start to take off, I looked into the sky as she took off and headed back towards the United States. *If it's meant to be, I'll see her again and until that day comes, I'll just have to live my life and never look back.*